Series Editor: Catherine Bowness

Growing Communities

The Work of Catherine Sneed

Vanessa

Illustrated by

The **Faith in Action** Series

RMEP

RELIGIOUS AND MORAL EDUCATION PRESS

GROWING COMMUNITIES

The Work of Cathrine Sneed

Cathrine lay helpless in her hospital bed. The chemotherapy was not helping – she was still very ill. 'Well, you're not responding,' the doctor told her, 'so you can go home to die, or you can stay here and die.'

Cathrine had been in and out of hospital with a rare form of kidney disease for almost a year. She had noticed how visitors were looking at her with sadness in their eyes and knew that they were sure she was dying.

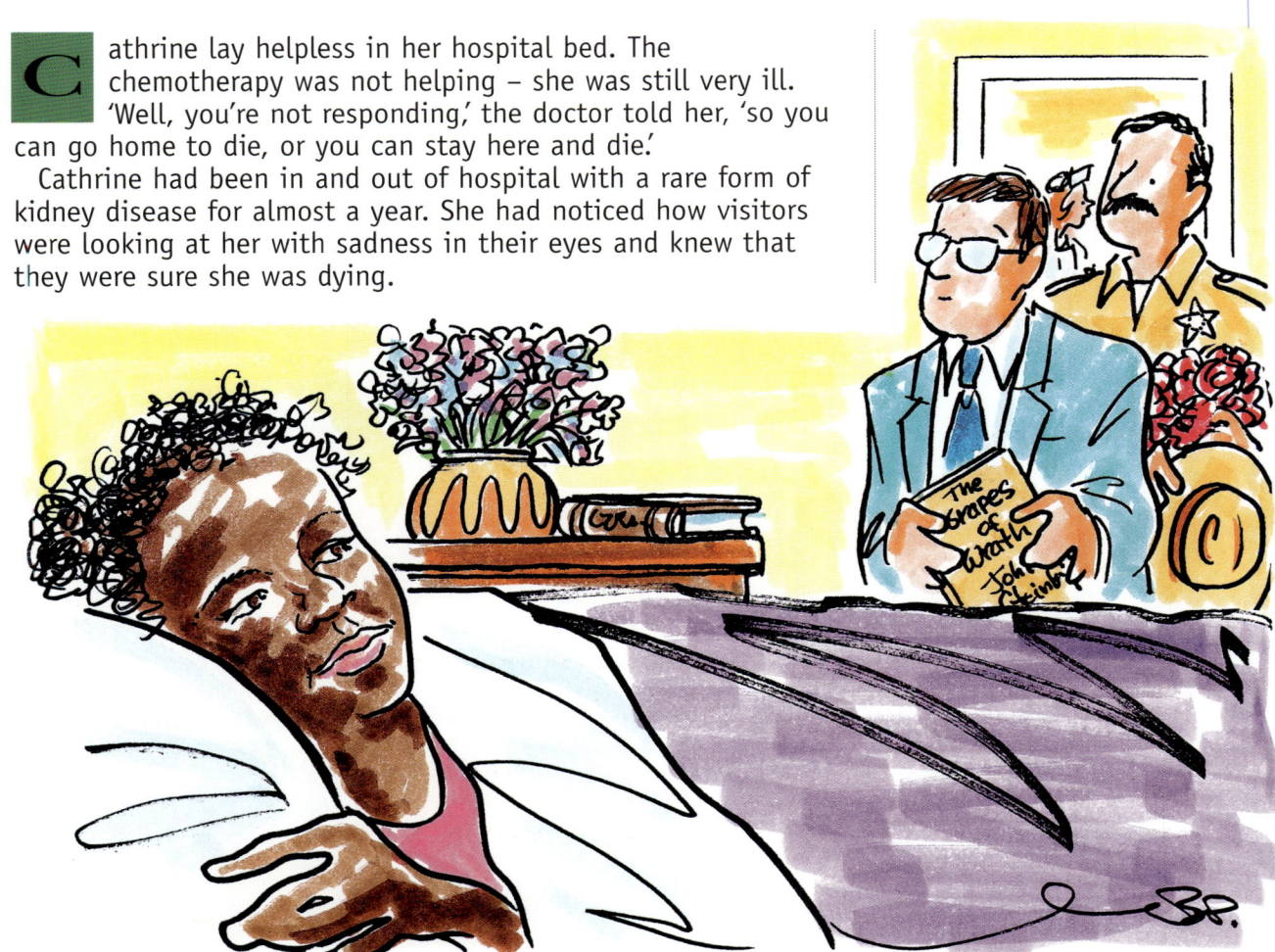

Cathrine's boss, Sheriff Michael Hennessey of San Francisco County, came to visit her and brought along Ray Towbis, his friend and chief of staff. Ray gave Cathrine a copy of John Steinbeck's novel *The Grapes of Wrath*. This book tells the story of people feeling helpless and losing their spirit when they had their land taken away from them. As she read the book Cathrine discovered a powerful message: if people who are feeling hopeless can connect with the land and continue feeling connected with it then it will give them hope and help them survive. It will give them faith in themselves. She could not get this message out of her head, 'Hope lies in the land and if we feel connected to the land then there is hope for us.'

The book had filled her with inspiration and when Michael and Ray next visited her she leapt out of the bed and declared she wanted to start a gardening project for the prisoners she supervised at the county jail. They received this news rather cautiously but how could Michael turn down the wishes of his dying colleague? Cathrine was discharged from hospital and immediately went back to work. She started to develop her new project when she could barely walk.

What Do You Think?

Important: In answering 'What Do You Think?' questions in this book, it is important that you not only state your opinion but also give as many reasons as possible for your opinion.

1. How do you think the hospital medical team reacted when Cathrine told them of her plans for a gardening project? Why?

2. What things may sometimes give people strength when they are very ill?

A Tough Start

Cathrine was born in Wiesbaden, Germany, in 1954, but she grew up in Newark, New Jersey in the United States of America. In 1971, when she was expecting her first child, she decided to hitchhike alone to San Francisco. One reason why she left Newark was because the local hospital had the highest number of infant deaths in the U.S.A., and she feared for her unborn baby. Hitchhiking hundreds of miles across America was a dangerous thing to do, though, and Cathrine was lucky to arrive in San Francisco unharmed.

The odds against survival for a pregnant 17-year-old African American were challenging. Often girls in a similar position ended up working as prostitutes and turned to drugs. As a result their children were taken away from them by the authorities because they could not look after them properly. Cathrine wanted to make more positive choices about her life and she felt that by going to San Francisco she could give her child a better start in life.

Growing Communities

To get enough money for food during the first few days in a new city, Cathrine sold the postage stamps her sister had given her to keep in touch. She lived with another sister and was soon able to claim food vouchers. Although these helped, they were not really enough, so she went to churches where they gave out bread and other 'luxuries' to the poor. Once her son was born she took him home on the bus wrapped in a blanket donated by a church. She also had some basic necessities such as towels, spoons and forks taken from the hospital and resolved to make her child's life a good one. So a few days later she re-started her college course and took her son in with her each day. Her partner joined her later and she had another child, a girl.

The father was a 23-year-old African American and despite having completed college he had very little chance of finding worthwhile work in the area. The two young people stayed together for many years trying to build a good life for their children and pursuing their own education, in law school, but went their separate ways later in life.

Cathrine puts a lot of her moral toughness and determination for a better life down to the fact that her father worked hard all his life. He was one of the very few African American officers in the United States Army and fought in both World War II and the Korean War. He had been willing to lay down his life for the nation and was awarded the Purple Heart for selfless bravery; however, as a black man he was still not entitled to vote in U.S.A. elections when he got home. Cathrine watched her father's gut determination in the face of such unfairness, pain and cruelty and learned to be strong. When he left the army in 1963, her father took a job with a government housing and urban development project and continued to work all his life.

Cathrine's mother died at 38 leaving nine children, so her father raised the children alone at first and then with his second wife and her three children. He told his children that school was all that could put them into a better situation. It was his views and words that kept Cathrine at school when friends dropped out. Cathrine's stepmother also influenced her, as she was active in politics at a time when women, and African American women in particular, rarely had a political voice.

It was at this time, in the late 1960s and early 1970s, that Civil Rights groups in America were pushing for social and political changes. There was much feeling that ordinary people really could bring about differences in areas where people were being treated wrongly by the system. Both Cathrine's father and her stepmother worked hard for a country that ultimately treated them poorly, but they had faith in it and the ability of its people to change.

Although Cathrine's own experiences help her to understand the difficulties faced by prisoners and their families, she is at pains to point out that she has always had a loving and supportive family. She believes it is this support which has given her the strength and courage to succeed.

What Do You Think?

1. Cathrine was only seventeen when she arrived in San Francisco. She went to the 'soup kitchen' at her church to get enough food to survive. She was in a very disadvantaged position, but then began to make her own choices about her future life. What do you hope to be doing at seventeen? What kinds of life choices might you face?

2. Cathrine's father was treated very badly by the United States Government after having fought for his country. Which do you think required more courage: fighting as a soldier or facing up to prejudice on his return home? Why?

3. Why did Cathrine's father believe education was Cathrine's only hope? Was he right? Give reasons.

Legal Training

Cathrine had always wanted to be a criminal lawyer and at twenty-one she joined the San Francisco Sheriff's Department, hoping to make sure that no one spent a minute longer than they should in jail. She began studying at New College School of Law and needed a place where her children could be safe whilst  she worked. Together with other mothers who wanted to study or work, she ran a children's crèche at the local church. She got funding for this by writing to charitable organizations, and was so successful that the crèche grew into a thriving nursery called Nkrumah School. Cathrine was the founder and director. The funds raised even paid for the church to be renovated.

Signs of Cathrine's leadership qualities in difficult situations were developing. Her success also meant that she had the chance to put something back into the church community which had given her food when she was in need. She realized the importance of gaining a sense of dignity by giving something back to those who have helped you in difficult times.

When Cathrine began to work in law she provided legal services for those who could not afford a lawyer then gradually became more interested in work related to murder and other serious crimes. She worked for lawyers, completed research projects and even spoke in court sometimes, which was a thrilling experience. Cathrine believed she was providing vital defence for those who were too poor to hire good lawyers. She was also very aware of how many more African American people compared with white people seemed to be arrested and prosecuted for crime.

She was once, however, shocked to discover clear evidence, in the form of bloody fingerprints, that a 19-year-old on 'Death Row', whom she had believed and defended, had indeed committed the murder. The lawyer she was working with pointed out that she should be representing her client whether or not she thought the person had committed the crime. She then realized that she did not want to do that. Her true aim was to get to the root cause of why people like her client, without any money or job, ended up in prison. She wanted to use this knowledge to help prevent this happening. She had seen so many similar teenagers who were poorly educated, unskilled and had no families facing criminal charges and a prison sentence. Cathrine believed that some of these young people had no real choices in their lives.

What Do You Think?

1. Why do you think there were so many young non-white people in United States prisons and on Death Row?

2. How far is it possible for people who are poor to resist peer pressure to be involved in crime?

A New Counselling Role

Cathrine began a course at law school called 'Prison Law'. The professor who taught it gave prisoners and released prisoners simple legal help with family matters such as divorce proceedings or fighting against eviction from their homes. The San Francisco County Jail at San Bruno had a very high level of prisoners committing suicide because of the terrible treatment they received from both prison guards and fellow prisoners, and because of the hopelessness of knowing what misery and poverty awaited them if and when they were released. On top of this Cathrine discovered that prisoners were behaving in a manner that showed they had lost the will to live and were fighting for no reason. They knew they had nothing to go back to when they finished serving their sentence so there was no reason to try to improve themselves. They were in a vicious circle where the prison guards would respond to their behaviour by treating them like animals and in response to this treatment the prisoners would feel they were worthless and behave in an even worse manner.

Cathrine's professor, Michael Hennessey, who later became sheriff of the city, was keen to make the prison humane and safe from the drugs and violence that plagued the place. Prisoners did not have any opportunity to transform and change their lives to create better futures for themselves when released; they were struggling to stay alive. Crime was very high in the prison and the life of a prisoner could be taken in exchange for drugs. One prisoner was beaten by another inmate for refusing to get off the phone and lay in a coma for five years till he died.

At the prison, criminals were simply being stored until release. Michael Hennessey wanted to turn this terrifying place into an environment where lives could be changed and prisoners could be equipped with skills and ideas that would help them build worthwhile lives. He had faith in Cathrine's ability to help and in 1982 he offered her the job of working as a counsellor who could talk with the prisoners about necessary changes to their lifestyle and then offer support whilst the changes were made. This would be her first full-time job with medical benefits for her and her children – Cathrine was delighted.

She started with the women prisoners and looked at their most basic but small needs which had previously been ignored. She arranged for the prisoners to have new clothes to wear when they were released. This meant that a woman who had served a sentence for prostitution did not have to leave prison in the clothes she had been wearing when she was arrested. Cathrine provided a bus ticket for each woman so that she could make one journey when she was set free. Also Cathrine discovered that by the time many women got out of prison their possessions had disappeared from their original hostels or homes. So she made collections of basic provisions for them and helped them find work and make a new start.

Many of the women prisoners were mothers and had been imprisoned for theft or prostitution. It struck Cathrine how like herself many of them were: mainly African American and poor, or poor Spanish-speaking immigrants or poor white people. The situation for these women was horrific. Not only were they sad because they were unable to be with their children, but they did not know who would care for their children nor how angry or upset their children might be with them for going to prison. Would their children ever even talk to them again?

The problems facing the non-English speakers were particularly challenging, as Cathrine discovered when she met a woman who had been greatly distressed since being arrested. No one knew why she was so upset until Cathrine found a Spanish-speaking priest to interpret. They discovered that she had been arrested for stealing in a supermarket, her baby had been taken from her on her arrest and she had not heard anything about it since. The priest found out for them that the child had been put into foster care. Cathrine located the baby and helped the mother regain custody after her release. However the baby was eventually taken into permanent care when the mother kept getting re-arrested. Short-term aid was clearly not going to be enough to help people who just went back to their old lives and patterns of behaviour on release from prison.

Since the early 1980s conditions and services for prisoners have begun to improve, but prisons in the U.S.A. remain very hard and dangerous places and still hold far more non-white prisoners than white ones. This must indicate that there are still huge underlying interconnected problems in society based on poverty, race and culture.

What Do You Think?

1. Why did the authorities so often overlook the basic needs of prisoners?

2. Why do many prisoners re-offend and serve one prison sentence after another?

3. Should the baby have been returned to its mother? What support could have been given to her to prevent her breaking the law again?

4. In prisons in the U.S.A. there are far more non-white prisoners that white prisoners. Do you agree that this indicates that there are still interconnected problems in society based on poverty, race and crime? Give reasons.

New Life from the Land

It was at this time of tension and stress from being around such desperate situations that Cathrine became seriously ill. Her kidneys, the organs which are supposed to cleanse the body of poisons and toxins, began to fail. Then Ray Towbis brought her the book *The Grapes of Wrath* to read whilst in hospital. As she read the story she realized that working with the land gives people a sense of self-worth and hope so that in the future they can make their lives better. The land gives people something they can connect with and care about beyond themselves.

She believed she had been called, that it was her mission to show people they could find faith in themselves through working on the land. There is, however, very little spare land in San Francisco and Cathrine had not done any real gardening before, but she felt she was called by the powerful message of the book. She was convinced that when we care and nurture something else, we are doing something for ourselves as well and this restores faith and confidence in the self. It is very healing. Prisoners become used to being told that they are worthless and cannot do anything of value and they begin to believe it. Cathrine wanted to teach them that growing plants successfully is useful and rewarding.

This was a turning-point in her life, a moment of insight and awakening at a spiritual and inspirational level. Ray made a tremendous impact on Cathrine's life and work and she says that he was her mentor and remains centrally important to the development of her life and work.

What Do You Think?

1. Re-read the description on pages 2–3 of Cathrine Sneed's moment of inspiration. Why does illness often cause people to reflect on their past and future lives?

2. What other people can you think of who experienced a key turning-point or moment of inspiration which changed their life? In what ways was their experience the same as or different from Cathrine's?

Growing Communities

A Prison Garden

Reading *The Grapes of Wrath* gave Cathrine a sense of purpose, and although she was so weak she could not even walk, she went straight to work on introducing the prisoners to the land. Her poor physical condition brought out gentler qualities in the prisoners and they would help her out to an old farm owned by the prison about half a mile away. Cathrine was soon impressed by the attitude of the female prisoners, who were enthusiastic to work day after day despite the demoralizing environment they went back to each evening. The prison guards thought she was mad and even placed bets on the likelihood of her being attacked by the prisoners – they offered her no support of any kind.

The women who had come into prison as prostitutes with false red fingernails now tore down old storage buildings with their bare hands. Male prisoners started coming out in work groups too and took an interest in the preparation of the land. It took two years for Cathrine to be able to walk properly again, but in that time a garden developed on the 3-hectare site. Cathrine's gardening knowledge was still only from books and people she talked into visiting the prison and giving advice. So she persuaded the sheriff to let her take time off to do courses. She spent a brief time studying in England but she missed her family life and returned to America to learn about organic vegetable growing on the Agro-Ecology Farm and Garden Programme at University College, Santa Cruz, so she could live at home. As Cathrine became more knowledgeable herself, she was able to pass on new skills to the prisoner gardeners.

Soon Cathrine had 120 prisoners growing free food for local soup kitchens in the three or four hours they were allowed out per day. This meant that for the first time the prisoner gardeners had meaningful work to do which provided something they could give away to others. In return people praised them and told them they had made something useful and beautiful. Cathrine also took prison vegetables to the city's poorest schools,

Prison Garden: Today's Jobs

- **Kitchen:** needs two diplomatic people who won't use the food for a power trip over the other prisoners.

- **Greenhouse:** five students to work with care and focus on planting, thinning out and watering seedlings.

- **Harvest:** six people to pick, clean, remove yellow leaves and package. We have grown thousands of dollars' worth of food here for the homeless. We send the best. Food is not charity, it's justice. Food is a human right.

- **Weeding:** fifteen people for weeding, which symbolizes the clearing out of problems, so that the plants can grow to their best ability. Your life is like the plant, you need to get the weeds out.

- **Compost:** a couple of students are needed to build and turn over the compost heap. Compost helps organic gardening. It's a symbol of turning mistakes into lessons.

- **Tree crew:** to weed around newly planted trees.

- **Bed preparation:** ten people to prepare beds for the seedlings to be transplanted into. It's like having a home to come to.

where the children were not allowed out at break because of the threat to health from used needles and condoms thrown into the playground. The pupils were thrilled to see food grown from seed and they screamed with excitement. Some were the children of the prisoners who had grown the crops and this made it particularly touching.

More than ten thousand prisoners have been through Cathrine's programme since it began in 1982. A typical day for the prisoner gardeners might include a list of jobs like the one on the coloured panel on the left. Cathrine's approach is positive, lively and fun, but demands that the prisoners have respect for themselves and others. This is the key to changing their way of life.

Arlene Hamilton, one of the teachers on Cathrine's programme, links gardening with her ideas about life for the prisoners. She says her seedlings sometimes look weak initially, but with care they grow and become healthier just like her prisoner students. She likens weeds to criminals and drug-dealers, saying that if you let them take root they will strangle you. Another favourite comparison of hers is that the task of watering a garden is like a person reporting to a police station, probation officer or social worker when on parole: they have to keep it up and not miss a single time.

Environmental artist Ned Kahn has collaborated with Cathrine to design a beautiful greenhouse which uses different-coloured glass panels to throw cobalt-blue and gold-yellow light over the prisoners and others working inside. Each day after their work, the team gathers in a room with quotations and posters of Martin Luther King and Gandhi, amongst others, lining the walls. They talk about what the project means to them or has done for them, how they are preparing for their own release and how they aim to maintain the freedom they will be given.

Arlene Hamilton also likes to use composting as a metaphor:

> Every troubled spot, every yellow leaf, can be turned back into productive soil.

So too with the lives of her prisoner students.

What Do You Think?

1. How might a child feel about a parent who is in serious trouble and serving a prison sentence?

2. How might having a parent in prison make a child feel about him- or herself? How might his or her feeling change if the parent did something responsible?

Growing Communities

Many prisoners working on Cathrine's gardening programme started to ask to stay longer in the jail instead of going back to the streets. One prisoner, a white man in his thirties called Danny, who had been an alcoholic and a drug-addict, did not want to leave prison at all. That was clearly not legal or possible so he was released; a couple of months later he was beaten to death on the streets. Whilst Danny had been growing vegetables in prison he had been changing, then it had all gone to waste when he was killed. That inspired Cathrine to find a way to keep ex-prisoners off the streets, where they might encounter crime and feel vulnerable.

If ex-prisoners try to get work they are often asked if they have ever been arrested. Employers are rarely willing to risk hiring a former criminal so they reject most ex-prisoners. This rejection adds to the person's feeling of worthlessness and means they lack the supportive environment they need to develop honest and fulfilling lives. When Cathrine looked at these people she was unsettled by how many of them were young African American men and women. She felt she must do something to help.

In 1992, Cathrine started a programme for ex-prisoners called the Garden Project, because she realized that they continued to need something to care for once they left prison. It had upset her greatly to discover that many released prisoners had been happy to come back to prison so that they could get back on her gardening programme. She had decided then that there needed to be a next stage so that the 'leavers' could move on. So, on Saturdays Cathrine and ex-prisoners started tree-planting in San Francisco. This way, however bad the week might have been for each person, they were accomplishing something together which gave them a sense of pride and self-respect. These people had often lost everything when they were in prison. Cathrine arranged some fund-raising so that ex-prisoners unable to afford the bus fare to a tree-planting site would receive the bus cash needed.

This was a great achievement, but Cathrine still didn't feel they were doing all they could. She tried to get sponsorship to develop the work and met the founder of the successful Just Deserts Bakery. He showed her a rubbish-tip behind his bakery and said he would not give her any money, but if they grew food on that land then he would buy that food from them. With the bakery and garden alongside each other, a partnership grew up between the garden and local business. Whilst the bakery bought strawberries from the garden for its patisseries, the gardeners could use the bakery toilets and eat up the baked goods not sold by the end of the day.

Many of the people working at the bakery garden were young parents and they could bring their children with them if they took their turn in minding the other children. This gave parents a break and also created a caring environment. The workers were paid $8–$11 (about £5–£8) per hour for two hours per day, but could stay on as unpaid volunteers for the rest of the day if they wished.

At first people said that no one would ever come and garden after leaving prison, but since then Cathrine has employed over three thousand former prisoners as staff at the Garden Project. She could afford to pay only 35 people at a time, but she could not bear to turn away weeping grown men so she ended up with about 125 workers, many of them volunteering their time just to be there. They gained a little food and the support of other former prisoners. Cathrine began a waiting list. The waiting list grew to more than two hundred.

From these humble beginnings, the Garden Project developed as it is today. It now produces so much food that whilst the emphasis is on giving food to soup kitchens and those who really need it, a small amount is sold to restaurants as well. But the project will never be a really commercial activity with fancy offices because it is designed to offer as many poor people as possible a chance to work and earn money and self-respect legally.

Garden Project participants are four times more likely to stay out of jail than ex-prisoners who have not been involved in the Garden Project.

What Do You Think?

1. Can a couple of hours a week spent on a worthwhile project be enough to change a life? Give reasons.

2. What support do you think should be offered to newly released prisoners? Should this support depend on the type of crime they committed or should everyone be given the same help to begin a new life?

3. Why did people choose to stay on at the garden and work for nothing?

Changing Lives through Organic Growing

The garden at the prison provides truckloads of organic food for the elderly, homeless, families in poverty and AIDS sufferers. Cathrine believes that the U.S.A. is spending huge amounts of money on keeping very poor people in prison, whereas if the State addressed the root cause of the crimes with adequate nutrition and employment leading to self-worth then those people would not be in prison. For every person sent to prison there is also a whole family and network behind that person that is affected. So a jail sentence may not only cost the State to keep that individual in prison, it may also mean that their family has to claim financial aid.

Cathrine also believes that the act of nurturing plants and growing food starts the process of criminals analysing the damaging effects on other people of what they have done. Workers at the garden training sites learn job skills, but more important, they learn life skills through the positive effect they have on the local environment and also on themselves. Both the garden behind the bakery and the garden at the prison are organically managed.

For Cathrine, poverty and drug-addiction are serious illnesses just like her own kidney disease. She says that in the same way that gardening has helped her health recover, it also helps heal prisoners' problems. She could not work with so many people on an individual level as a counsellor, but the gardens help her by supporting them all. She says the participants can see God is there with them in the garden, manifested in both the plants and the planters.

Most of the food is given away because that encourages the participants to care about other people and also about themselves. On the project, they learn about health and nutrition and the importance of caring about themselves. Most of the people Cathrine sees say that at the time of their arrest they placed no importance on eating well or in the home, but were more likely to go for high-fat and low-nutrition fast food whenever they had any money. She believes that it is possible to change how people feel about themselves and their lives and how they consequently behave, if they can be shown the advantages of home-cooked fresh organic food shared within the home. The experience of growing, preparing and cooking encourages the development of a caring and nurturing attitude.

Cathrine also encourages people in the community to come and see what the project workers are doing so that they can feel part of it and will respond more positively to the participants' attempts to improve their lives. The project participants tend to feel very badly about the crimes they have committed and the ways they have treated others in the past in order to pay for their drugs habit or survive without work. The project gives them a second chance to earn respect and feel a sense of self-worth.

Initially, Cathrine had found many of the prison staff unsupportive and mocking as the culture of most U.S.A. jails is to 'lock them up and throw away the key'. Her approach is one of rehabilitation so that the prisoners and ex-prisoners can be brought back into productive roles in society. A sergeant at San Francisco County Jail prefers the 'tough on the criminal' line, but has developed a respect for Cathrine's gardening programme. He says,

> [Its participants] don't have the institutionalized jail mind. They develop more self-awareness and are more willing to hold themselves accountable for what they did and what they don't want to repeat.

He sees how participants move from a position of believing they are in prison because the police caught them to addressing the fact that they are in prison because they have been drug-dealing or have committed other crimes mostly involving theft or violence. This is a necessary stage of recognition before they are able to tackle the problem.

The law-enforcement staff at the prison are notorious for high rates of divorce, alcoholism and suicide owing to the stressful nature of their work. Cathrine sees how the motivation and enthusiasm of the ex-prisoners gives the prison guards more hope as well. For Hallowe'en in 1998, the prisoners grew over a thousand pumpkins to take to local schools. The ex-prisoners, police and prison guards who delivered the huge pumpkins to the happy shrieking children, many of whom had never seen a pumpkin before, said it was the moment that meant the most to them in their whole careers. The prison guards now receive vegetables from the prisoner gardeners and have started to be more supportive.

There is a deep bond of friendship and affection at the Garden Project, the prison garden and the Tree Corps. Cathrine Sneed calls those who excel in their time at the Garden Project the 'stars' and ten of them have now formed the Tree Corps, which plants trees in low-income areas of the city. More than 10 000 trees have been planted by the corps on the streets of San Francisco, mostly in areas where there were none before. The workers earn $8 (£5–£6) per hour, which is not much, but the rewards of teamwork, being out in the fresh air and growing something that future generations will enjoy are far greater. The philosophy of greening the city and community is central to Cathrine's whole approach and the corps are even learning the plant names in Latin. Cathrine also reads to her students from inspiring books about people's connection to the land when working on it.

What Do You Think?

1. Cathrine says, 'The people working with me – some of them with sixty-five, seventy criminal convictions – can feed people. And while they're feeding people, they're feeding themselves, and they're creating new communities. They're creating hope in their communities.' What do you think she means?

2. Cathrine argues that vast amounts of money are spent on keeping a particular kind of prisoner in jail, people who have committed crimes mainly because they are very poor. She wants prisoners to work in and with the community to heal the wounds that they created. Would this idea work with all types of prisoner? Give some examples and some reasons for your point of view.

3. Cathrine says, 'Growing food and giving the food to these places [soup kitchens, centres for the elderly and community centres] has helped to restore the prisoners and the participants in the program because they're able to give something. They're able to give of themselves.' What similar projects could be set up to help prisoners?

4. Discuss how important it may be to the transformation of the prisoners' attitudes that their labour in the garden is not used to save money or make a profit for the prison, but that vegetables are given free of charge by the prisoners directly to the needy.

Making a Difference

Cathrine Sneed still runs gardening and planting programmes in San Francisco. She has transformed the lives of prisoners and former prisoners, reduced the rate of prisoners re-offending, produced organic produce for some of the San Francisco Bay Area's leading restaurants and markets, and provided a model for law-enforcement officials. Her work has given many people a real way out of the seemingly endless cycle of crime and poverty. By offering participants in her projects the opportunity of education, some regular food and a little income, she gives them the chance to develop themselves and find even more work. She tells a moving story about crying uncontrollably at her daughter's graduation because she remembered queuing to get her some bread at a soup kitchen and now her daughter was in a position to help others who were suffering. She sees a clear connection between her own self-esteem and the fact that she always had work, and believes both those things were crucial in her own children succeeding in their lives.

The United States Department of Agriculture gave the Garden Project the following glowing praise, describing it as 'one of the most innovative and successful community-based crime prevention programs in the country. But its value goes far beyond crime prevention, providing job training, employment, environmental appreciation and beautification – often for the first time – for people and places in need.'

Cathrine's job and life-skills programmes run during and after prison sentences offer a unique combination of inspiration, education and actual practical work yielding immediate results. She actively encourages others to learn from her work and adapt parts of her programmes for their own communities. Guides on this have now been produced and similar projects have been set up in a number of areas. It is hoped that the work will continue to spread and change the lives of countless other individuals.

How often are people told that it is not worth taking a stand or showing their feelings as it will not make any difference to society, because one person has only one small and powerless voice? Cathrine Sneed knows how untrue this is as she has seen the impact that one vegetable garden has had. She was inspired to start work at a local level without much money, but that small project has offered hope for a new start to thousands of prisoners and ex-prisoners. She believes people must say, 'We're going to start very small, and we're going to do what we can with what we've got.' She thinks we have to start by using examples that are good and build on them.

Many participants in her gardening programmes have said that Cathrine Sneed changed their lives. Comments include:

> I get peace of mind.

> I like it because I see a beginning and an end. You put [the seed/plant] in, see it grow, and harvest it.

> If you can take this lesson with you, gentlemen, you won't be back.

Cathrine says she only gave them the garden, which taught them to have the faith in themselves to change their own lives.

Biographical Notes

1954	Born in Wiesbaden, Germany.
1963	Father retires from U.S. Army. Family now living in Newark, New Jersey, U.S.A.
1971	Cathrine hitches to San Francisco to have her first baby at a safer hospital and raise it in a city that offered more than Newark could.
1975	Founds a crêche so that she can do her legal training and so that other mothers can also go to work and study. This becomes Nkrumah School, of which she is founder and director.
1982	Joins the San Francisco Sheriff's Department as a counsellor.
1982	Sets up the Horticulture Project for San Francisco County Jail inmates on 3 hectares of land.
1992	Becomes Special Assistant to the Sheriff in the San Francisco Sheriff's Department. Founder and director of the Garden Project, for ex-prisoners.
1996	Visits Great Britain to give Schumacher Lecture in Bristol.

Cathrine Sneed has received many awards for her work, including the California State Assembly Certificate of Recognition, National Foundation for the Improvement of Justice Award, M.F.K. Fisher Award for ground-breaking work with food and the Hero for the Earth Award.

Things to Do

1 Imagine that a seventeen-year-old arrives alone in your nearest town when she is about to give birth to a baby. Research all the places where she may be able to find help and support and write a simple guide telling her where to go and what to do.

2 Cathrine Sneed's gardening programmes have helped to rehabilitate prisoners in America. Using the Internet or other resources, find out about rehabilitation projects for prisoners in your country. Make a presentation, adding further suggestions of your own.

3 Imagine an elderly person comes to the Garden Project and meets a young person who has served a prison sentence for stealing a purse from another senior citizen. Write the script of a conversation between the young ex-prisoner and the elderly person.

4 Create an advertisement or poster asking for volunteers to work as mentors for prisoners. List the qualities the volunteers must have and explain what they might be asked to do.

5 Imagine you are trapped in a place and way of life which offers you no hope for the future and no role in life. Write a poem or compose a piece of music to illustrate how you feel about yourself and about the people around you.

6 Make a radio programme showing how Cathrine Sneed's life experience plays a role in making prisoners and ex-prisoners more willing to listen to and learn from her.

7 Invite a prison visitor to school and ask them to tell you about their voluntary work inside prison.

8 In what ways does the Garden Project offer support to the participants? Imagine that you have been given the funding to develop a project which would offer support to people who have just left prison or other long-term care. Write a description of your project, showing how it would help re-integrate its participants into modern society.

Growing Communities

Questions for Assessment or Examination Candidates

9 (a) Outline Christian teaching linked to the phrase 'I was in prison and you visited me.' (5 marks)

(b) What does 'rehabilitation' mean? (5 marks)

(c) Why do some religious people believe that prison should be for rehabilitation rather than for punishment? (10 marks)

10 (a) Describe a turning-point in the life of a religious believer you have studied. (5 marks)

(b) Explain how their life changed direction after this point. (5 marks)

(c) Some people believe that God's influence is behind all their life-changing experiences and that this is how they find their true vocation. With reference to any religion you have studied, show how this view may be justified. (10 marks)

11 'People who are in prison deserve to be there. Prisons are not holiday-camps, they are for punishment.'

Some religious believers would disagree with this statement but some might agree. For each point of view, give an argument to show how it might be justified by referring to religious texts you have studied. (10 marks for each argument)

Religious and Moral Education Press
A division of SCM-Canterbury Press Ltd,
a wholly owned subsidiary of
Hymns Ancient & Modern Ltd
St Mary's Works, St Mary's Plain
Norwich, Norfolk NR3 3BH

Copyright © 2002 Vanessa Gray

Vanessa Gray has asserted her right under the Copyright, Designs and Patents Act, 1988, to be identified as Author of this Work.

All rights reserved. No part of this publication may be reproduced, stored in a retrieval system, or transmitted, in any form or by any means, electronic, electrostatic, magnetic tape, mechanical, photocopying, recording or otherwise, without permission in writing from the publishers.

First published 2002

ISBN 1 85175 260 9

Designed and typeset by
TOPICS – The Creative Partnership,
Exeter

Cover illustration by Jane Taylor

Printed in Great Britain by
Brightsea Press, Exeter for
SCM-Canterbury Press Ltd, Norwich

Notes for Teachers

The first Faith in Action books were published in the late 1970s and the series has remained popular with both teachers and pupils. However, much in education has changed over the last twenty years, such as the development of both new examination syllabuses in Religious Studies and local agreed syllabuses for Religious Education which place more emphasis on pupils' own understanding, interpretation and evaluation of religious belief and practice, rather than a simple knowledge of events. This has encouraged us to amend the style of the Faith in Action Series to make it more suitable for today's classroom.

The aim is, as before, to tell the stories of people who have lived and acted according to their faith, but we have included alongside the main story questions which will encourage pupils to think about the reasons for the behaviour of our main characters and to empathize with the situations in which they found themselves. We hope that pupils will also be able to relate some of the issues in the stories to other issues in modern society, either in their own area or on a global scale.

The 'What Do You Think?' questions may be used for group or class discussion or for short written exercises. The 'Things to Do' at the end of the story include ideas for longer activities and more-structured questions suitable for assessment or examination practice.

In line with current syllabus requirements, as Britain is a multifaith society, Faith in Action characters will be selected from a wide variety of faith backgrounds and many of the questions may be answered from the perspective of more than one faith.

CMB, 1997

Acknowledgements

The author would like to thank Cathrine Sneed for her kind help with this book, the Schumacher Society for providing Cathrine's lecture transcript, and Allan Spalding for support and encouragement.